H is for Haiku

A Treasury of Haiku from A to Z

by Sydell Rosenberg
Illustrated by Sawsan Chalabi

Penny Candy Books
Oklahoma City & Savannah

The Sustainable Forestry Initiative® program integrates the perpetual growing and harvesting of trees with the protection of wildlife, plants, soils and water.

"On What Is Haiku" was first published in *Wind Chimes*, Number 3, 1981.
Photo of Sydell Rosenberg & Amy Losak by Sam Rosenberg (1961)
Photo of Sawsan Chalabi by Sandy Major Photography

Cover design, illustrations & lettering: Sawsan Chalabi, schalabi.com
Book design: Shanna Compton, shannacompton.com

22 21 20 19 18 1 2 3 4 5
ISBN-13: 978-0-9987999-7-1 (hardcover)

Books for the kid in *all* of us
www.pennycandybooks.com

Dear Reader,

A green weed grows in a sidewalk crack. A sparrow splashes in a puddle near the curb. Pigeons gather on a high window ledge. The rush and rumble of our daily lives. What do these things have in common?

They are all examples of simple, "small" moments. Thousands of small moments surround us. We see, hear, smell, taste, and touch them every day.

Often, we don't give them a second thought because they don't stand out. Or we may be too busy or too distracted to take notice. But these small moments can become a short form of poetry called haiku. Haiku poems make small moments "big."

The haiku poems in this book were all written by my mother, Sydell Rosenberg, many years ago. She was a public school teacher in New York City, and she loved to write about her experiences.

Syd, as we called her, was one of the first members of the Haiku Society of America, and it was her dream to publish a book of haiku for children. In the note that follows, Syd offers her explanation of what haiku can be.

Haiku poems originated in Japan as a way to observe the seasons and our natural world. English interpretations of the form have traditionally featured 3 lines with 5 syllables on the first line, 7 on the second line, and 5 on the last line. But many haiku writers aren't so strict about syllable counts or the subject matter, including Syd.

What's most important about writing haiku is to focus on those many small moments we may overlook and make them special.

—Amy Losak

What Is Haiku?

Now I go to what is there, and each time, get
something different. Sometimes I get what I want—and
other times, perhaps more rewarding, I get what I didn't
know I didn't want, with pain. Each time, discovery.

Haiku is that fledgling moment, when
the wingstrokes become sure—when the
bird has staying power in the air.

Haiku can't be gimmicked; it can't be shammed. If it is
slicked into cuteness, haiku loses what it had to give.

The split second one starts to touch a
flower—real or plastic? That's haiku. Before
the hoof comes down—that's haiku!

—Sydell Rosenberg

ADVENTURES OVER
THE CAT SITS
IN THE FUR RING
OF HIS TAIL, AND DREAMS

BOY ON A
MAILBOX
PERCHED LIKE A
SOLITARY BIRD
WATCHING
THE
SUN SET

U.S.
MAIL

CAR BURIED IN SNOW—
ON BACK SEAT,
A WIDE-EYED DOLL
READY FOR A JAUNT

RAIN
CLANKING
DROPS
OF
WATER
INTO
AN
OLD
CAN
TO
RUST
LEFT
OUTSIDE

EVEN IN THE AIR
WITH A BERRY IN HIS MOUTH—
BLUE JAY CAW-CAWING

FIRST LIBRARY CARD
AND A PROMISE TO READ ALL
AUTHORS A TO Z

Gleaming in Profile
Spoiling its own Camouflage—
The Iguana's Eye

HOLDING UMBRELLAS
CHILDREN, LIKE ROWS
OF MUSHROOMS,
GLISTEN
IN THE
RAIN

IN A FISH WINDOW
"MONSTERS!" THE CHILDREN EXCLAIM—
GREEN LOBSTERS
WRITHING

JUMPING QUIETLY
THE CAT FOLLOWS A PEACH PIT
TOSSED FROM THE TERRACE

KEEPING
THEIR DISTANCE
FROM THE HOOVES
OF THE HORSES —
PIGEONS AND
SPARROWS

LAKE
WATER
MELTING
THE LEGS
OF THE
FLAMINGOS
WADING
IN THE
SUN

MUNCHING ON ACORNS
A SQUIRREL SWEEPS
UP SUNBEAMS
WITH HER TRANSPARENT
TAIL

NEON WINGS OF MOTH
EXPLODING INTO HEADLIGHTS
ON A COUNTRY ROAD

ON A RUBY SUN
TWO WHITE SWANS CROSS THEIR BLACK BEAKS
AS THEY MEET,
GLIDING

PLUNGING DOWNHILL
PETALS FALLING IN HER HAIR—
GIRL ON A BIKE

QUEUING FOR
ICE CREAM-
SWEAT-SPRINKLED
OFFICE WORKERS
ON QUEENS
BOULEVARD

Room of First-Graders Practicing the Recorder Through a Thunderstorm

SO PALE – IT HARDLY SAT ON THE OUTSTRETCHED BRANCH OF THE WINTER NIGHT

TURNING AND
TURNING
THEIR HEADS WITH RAGGED PETALS—
ROADSIDE SUNFLOWERS

UP AND DOWN THE BLOCK
HOMEOWNERS MATE THE COVERS
OF GUSTED TRASH CANS

VACATION COTTAGE
LONG JOHNS ON A MOUNTAIN TOP
SWAYING IN THE SUN

WHEN THE SU
CAME OUT
MY TURTLE CLIMBED
ON A ROCK
AND CONJURED
A VIEW

XAVIER IS BACK
IN THE BEAUTY PARLOR—
"WHO IS XAVIER?"

YESTERDAY'S COOL RAIN
LEFT THIS FLAT PUDDLE SMOOTHING
THE WRINKLED LEAVES

ZUM ZUM RESTAURANT–
A FRENCH TEACHER
GRADES PAPERS
ON HER LUNCH BREAK

Sydell Rosenberg (1929–1996) lived, wrote, and taught in New York City. Syd was a charter member of the Haiku Society of America in 1968 and served as HSA's Secretary in 1975. Her short poems—notably haiku and senryu, including some in this book—were published in various magazines and anthologies, such as *American Haiku; Haiku Magazine*; *Frogpond*; *Wind Chimes*; *Modern Haiku*; *Haiku West*; *Haiku Highlights*; *The Haiku Anthology*; *The Haiku Handbook: How to Write, Share, and Teach Haiku*; *Haiku World: An International Poetry Almanac*; *The Teachers & Writers Handbook of Poetic Forms*; *Poets Anonymous*; and more. One of Syd's "city haiku" was included in the delightful urban public art project, "Haiku on 42nd Street" in 1994, in which the marquees of shuttered movie theaters in Times Square—the "Crossroads of the World"—were transformed into showcases for micropoetry. She also published prose and literary/word puzzles. Syd received her MA in English as a Second Language from Hunter College in 1972. She was married to Sam Rosenberg (d. 2003) for more than forty years. Their children are Amy Losak, married to Cliff, and Nathan Rosenberg, married to Deborah. Their grandchildren are Zachary and Julia.

Sawsan Chalabi is a Lebanese-American illustrator and designer. She earned her MFA in Illustration from Savannah College of Art and Design. When she is not at her computer making digital illustrations, she can be found in her studio getting messy with inks and paint. She loves applying subtle wit and humor in her pieces. Her work has been published by the *Washington Post*, *Cricket*, *Bust*, *Wine & Spirits*, *Applied Arts*, Penguin, and Lee & Low Books, among others. She currently resides in Washington, DC, where she continues to explore the power in the silent communication of art.